She Heads into the Wilderness

She
Heads
into the
Wilderness

ANNE MARIE
MACARI

Autumn House Press

PITTSBURGH

"Autumn House" and "Autumn House Press" are registered trademarks
owned by Autumn House Press, a nonprofit corporation whose mission
is the publication and promotion of poetry and other fine literature.

Autumn House Press Staff
Executive Editor and Founder: Michael Simms
Executive Director: Richard St. John
Community Outreach Director: Michael Wurster
Co-Director: Eva-Maria Simms
Fiction Editor: Sharon Dilworth
Coal Hill Editor: Joshua Storey
Associate Editors: Anna Catone, Laurie Mansell Reich,
   Rebecca Clever, Philip Terman
Special Projects Manager: Courtney Lang
Assistant Editor: Bernadette James
Editorial Consultant: Ziggy Edwards
Media Consultant: Jan Beatty
Tech Crew Chief: Michael Milberger

ISBN: 978-1-932870-24-4
Library of Congress Control Number: 2008929874

All Autumn House books are printed on acid-free paper and meet the
international standards of permanent books intended for purchase by libraries.

For Joan Larkin & Jean Valentine

Acknowledgments

Alaska Quarterly: from "Their Eyes Were Opened" XII

American Poetry Review: "Earth Elegy"; "Praying Mantis"; "Steller's Sea Cow"; from "Their Eyes Were Opened" XIX–XXVIII

The Beloit Poetry Journal: "Mozart's *Requiem*"

The Cortland Review: from "Their Eyes Were Opened" III–VI

Dirty Napkin: from "Their Eyes Were Opened" VII, VIII

FIELD: from "Their Eyes Were Opened" XXXIII–XXXVI

The Great River Review: "The Changing Coat"'; "My Lost Needle"

Night Sun: "Ants"; "Migration South"

Third Coast: "American Tree Sparrow, Platte River, Nebraska"; from "Their Eyes Were Opened" XV–XVI

Tiferet: "Horses"

Contents

ONE *Earth Elegy*

TWO *Their Eyes Were Opened*

THREE *Epilogue*

_____ **ONE**

Earth Elegy

Earth Elegy

By the time it fell, the tree was already part rot,
eaten by termites and ants,

stained with rain and urine, colonized. For years
I watched from my kitchen

as it ungathered in leaves and needles,

bleached, dissolving, though I hardly noticed
how the slow orgy

of weather took it season after season
into the pelvic

trench of dirt, and I got used to seeing it
pointing down the hill

like a giant's fibrous arm
soft with fungus.

We'd kick it to see the wood crumble, see
the insects, horrible kinds,

writhe out of its cracks. And once I read that our air
is full of life we can't see

and thought of the sky falling with the falling tree,

and disintegrating with the tree, a company
of beings, billions,

dying as we were dying and other beings driving
through the debris

and living off it—the dining and dead together,
unseen, spinning and tilted

like us on our axis, pitched toward some
ever-place

of crashing trees, ravenous creatures,
the dirt lit

with their living-dying backbones.

_____ Migration South

Early morning along the river, animals pulsing
but motionless—

like the Indigo Bunting resting its small blue body
on a stalk of sorghum,

its head turned west in contemplation. All day
hiking, canoeing, finding

what we could—a Jesus Lizard, crowned, with feet
so fast it could walk on water

if it weren't frozen there trying to look
like a stick, or the Spider Monkey

leaping between trees, arms and legs splayed wide
overhead so it seemed

held still in space. That night, exhausted, I dimmed
the lights, relieved to be alone,

as if I hadn't been able to think all day with
so much life around me, till

in my half-sleep I heard rough wing-beats, not bird

but a harder rasping, and turned to face a cockroach size
of a flattened hen's egg

scurrying behind a cabinet. Up in the thatched roof
I imagined colonies of insects

watching over me, invisible multitude,
and who was I to question them?

Who was I with my binoculars and books?

Not the Hissing Roach or Dusky Antbird, not
a shelled thing with wings

that clicked when it moved, but a frightened
creature of the north,

out of her habitat, no feeble quills on my back,
no gliding from the tree,

just that same falling and falling again, startled

into my bed, into my own featherless skin. Overhead:
clouds of tiny creatures,

the eyes of roaches, moths, broken arm
of the bat, or a bird

trapped in the peaked roof, frantic for release.

_____ **August**

Shells lined up on the table, some smaller than
a baby's fingernail and almost

as translucent, conch shells, spirals twisted
the way trees on cliffs

twist in battering wind. And look, dry
tissue corpses of insects

blown into corners, one discarded house after another.

Late summer, wasps circling a silver dome. Sometimes
I too spiral in a dream, turning

within myself, swimming inside. Like the woman
struggling to speak, saying

this pain, it's not real, not real—so I saw

her circling, rubbing against air like a snake
slipping out of its skin, the atmosphere

salty as the sea, and she drifting

away from me, though I remember her face,
the pale shell of it trying to smile,

and how it floated there in its agony,

floated free for a moment, her eyes like the curves
inside the conch where we can't see

unless we break it, shatter its intricate life, its crook
of dark. Late summer,

all that was made I undo:

hose down the wasp nest, pick honeycombs
off the eaves, pinch

the rusty faces of flowers, throw stones at the waves,
lose the shells in pockets and

straw bags, turn away, the season

rounding its corner, wind whipping my face.
Not real, she said, *what I do*

to get through the day. Shake out blankets,

bang sand from a shoe. A winding down
into the belly, grooves

deepening on skin or shell, floating things
hoisted, sunk, then spun loose

and dragged along the shore.

_____ From the Plane

It is a soft thing, it has been sifted
from the sieve of space and seems
asleep there under the moths of light.

Cluster of dust and fire, from up here
you are a stranger and I am dropping
through the funnel of air to meet you.

_____ Ants

An endless trail of leaf-cutter ants passed
before our feet and our guide Luis

told me how one had sliced
his skin in the cradle

between his thumb and second finger,
and how long it took to heal.

And like the temples and palaces
of Tikal I could imagine being

cut into some mosaic of myself, broken
by the ants into small bits

of green and brown and carried piecemeal
over the grass, my life

given over to a love of nothing in particular,
a scattering; I don't know how

he got to the subject of the Milky Way,
a road in the middle

parting the white silk of space, as if

the ants led there, through the trees,
down to earth,

then back up—all those small green
trapezoids of grief

filling the void—or why I thought about
kissing, how we could

dissolve ourselves, practicing through
our mouths for the next life,

as the stones on the temples so slowly, thoroughly,
pressed against each other,

as the heat and dampness pressed
my eyelids and drummed

my chest. So much ruining us,
as we are meant

to be ruined. The frame
collapsing. My hand raised toward

your face, your eyes
closing.

Mozart's *Requiem*

That night in Prague I dreamed singing, *lacrimosa*,
windows open, voices

crossing paths, a chorus bearing him
even as he wanted

to stay, dying and composing
as the untongue licked him

toward oblivion and the tenors sang *promisisti*.

And woke to the feeling of being *there* and *there*
swept up and

plunged back. I lay still in the record heat

listening for the atmosphere to change, almost
feeling it, hundreds of miles off

but coming this way. As sometimes hearing
the music, far off

but approaching, voices thin at first,
making room

for *sanctus*, mouth open even if
I'm full of dread,

even if beyond Mozart's death there's
one Napoleon after another—

visionaries with their frozen dead.

There's the music and there's
the marching, *Rex tremendae*,

and someone, *majestatis*, paying the price,
car bombs, body bags,

and now they play music in their helmets,
supplicanti,

such blessings the morning after
hearing his *Requiem*,

the music, *lux perpetua*, that has everything,
even terror, how believing

when I hear it, almost too beautiful to be
human voices, knowing it

so well and wanting to sing
all the parts, a kind

of purification, a prayer, like the story of him

still composing when he died—as if without
agony—music all over

the bed, last contractions, timpani, cellos,
his ink-stained hands.

Certain Sparrow

There's a certain sparrow fought for
by two males. All day long they mate,
taking turns—all day long
sperm flying, spilling
as the few inches of herself skirt
the trees and the small stripes
of her wings blur, leaving streaks
of this sadness or that.

We met in a strange world, in a frenzy.
A spiral of ups and downs.
Didn't I feel the lit orb, inside and out?
Later, I returned to the calcium
of loneliness, the fine shell spotted and cracked,
and the delicate thing ticking inside.

———— Ireland

Since then the mute grasses   long
            and sloping   sun-striped
I grow hunched and quiet with them
            swept by the fur
of banked clouds   not your country
            I tell myself   as if
I could know any place   as if I were
            in a place but am not
really   that is the happiness
            the grasses sing

Praying Mantis

The praying mantis rests on
my green towel near
the open window, each distinct part
like a child's wooden toy.

My son carries it to the sill overlooking
the yard. The mantis moves gently
like a creature in love,
though I have seen one devour

a grasshopper slowly—grasshopper
half in, half out, of its mouth—
stick arms lifted up
to its mandibles. Maybe grace

is what we do without hatred.
Grace doesn't need us.
It is silent as the mantis, head bowed
and mouth moving as if

it wanted for nothing as it waits
to impale an insect—
even a hummingbird—with the spines
of its forelegs. The first chill

of September settles around
the house, which for this moment
is the house grace made, in which
for this moment we have

no hatred for each other, only
a constant hunger
that is our way of moving
through the world. O mantis,

Christ child. Your six legs
a cradle: inside
your long thorax,
your abdomen, rocking.

_____ Horses

When the horses ran up and over
the hill, when they disappeared as though
they were entering some world beyond me,
separate and separately blessed, in which
a mare prophesied and a foal
lay quiet in the straw,

When one lifted his head into the appled-
branches, and the odor coated
his flaring nostrils and filmed
his eyes, and love made his flanks
quiver, and he tried but could not
shake such love out of his black body,

When a horse stood alone in the field,
still as a house, looking first down toward
the dry grass, then up, stamping
her hoof, but silent, too proud,
knowing her beauty cast her
into a world of greed and worshippers
in which she would never be known
to praise or bow down,

When the horses turned and galloped
shyly toward the man in the truck who was
the only one who became a horse when he touched
their heads, scolded them, who knew
their eyes to carry such history, such memory,
as could shame us all which was why

they were introverted and sometimes
angry, why they shook their heads
and why there was always a zealot
among them—backing off,
rearing up, fervid for truth.

_____ The Shrew

The shrew I almost trampled
and the wind it made near my foot,
and the stone stair it dashed across—
I never saw it coming, small boat,
night-ferry. Tonight I'm adrift,
I have not the shroud of hair, the life inside
and under, the gnawing and digging, the closeness.
Without you, I can't find my own skin.
I should have listened for
its retreating feet, I should have parted
the ferns and called out its name.

American Tree Sparrow, Platte River, Nebraska

Out here hunger takes shape as
a coyote crossing the white field,
or a crane dancing in the frozen
corn stubs. There's no end to beaks
stabbing ice: yellow legs, snipe, pintails,
and hunkered together in the river
cranes by the thousands rising
through the snow in one gray wave
to forage bony fields. Even memory's
a kind of hunger, wanting to go back
just once, as if this white scrim
of a world could be lifted and the past
in its fullness would be there behind
this ashy afterlife, this snow-blotted
landscape where sky and earth weld, no crack
between them.   When he holds out
the bird in his open hand, dead on
the roadside, car-swiped searching
for food, I almost believe it could
be quickened till he slowly spreads
the fan of its wing and I see how
its rufus-capped head is twisted
all wrong, how its eyes have no use
for light. Who will feast on it when
he lays it back on the snowbank? Who
will rip its delicate breast? Brief fill
for the hungry hole, brief passage
through the secret place, brief life, fast death.
Out here, the mother of beaks and talons
is always eating and I am like
those starving birds flashing their red
bellies and yellow chests, flailing
as anything approaches, crying, *eat me,*
eat me, mother, for I feel useless

some days in this life. Hook my throat, wear
the silk of my blood on your face. Tell me
there was a reason, more than hunger,
that drove me here. Then leave of me
what's left, scattered on the roadside,
for there are so many travelers
and they are forever hungry.

_____ Steller's Sea Cow

Even as they killed them
to extinction, the sea cows
drifted and swam in arctic waters
unafraid of the stranded men.

In the sea cows' parables it was foretold
that extinction comes
into the mind before the body,
a kingdom of oblivion

to swim toward, like the last
passenger pigeon perched
in a zoo, forgetting how
to fly, or a sea cow

slaughtered and dragged to shore, the last
of its kind in the frozen strait—
toothless, spearless,
as the day it was made

but too big to hide. Now they are
parables of themselves
floating in the bloodstreams of humans
who don't even know

they are haunted, followed by sea cows
who watch them as clouds
watch the ocean where the creatures
lived, or by passenger pigeons

who fly into memory, zigzagging
overhead like invisible
schools of fish. _Come children_,
the great mammals whisper,

find yourselves in the family
of man among the giants
of history. And she who writes
about the lost sea cow,

tell her the air she moves in
is singed with extinction.
We are waiting. Remember how
we turned the other cheek?

The world is never
alone, it was never alone.

_____ **TWO**

Their Eyes Were Opened

_____ **Their Eyes Were Opened**

I   (We Always Ate from That Tree)

We always ate from that tree. The women
with child craved its fruit, sweetest, most red.

The way she held it that day, and pressed it to
her cheek like a pillow, and slowly slit it with

her teeth, and ate it while rubbing her sore
back against the tree like a horse. Then many

of them rushing her, screaming she was unclean,
pushing her into the dirt like a serpent where

she writhed from them, where they taught her right from
wrong and when they were done they bound and covered

her outlaw breasts, her spirit garden below.
And they threw the fruit of the tree to the animals

and smashed the clay figures. And it went on
like that, beyond memory, on and on.

II *(On and On)*

On and on, finally believing she
had caused it. That all along they'd warned her,

holy tree, holy fruit, and the One so good
and what had she done? Trespass and dirt

became her, and food rotted in her throat.
No penance enough, no bowing, groveling,

no covering up, no pleasing the One who
loved her anyway despite it all.

And still obedience came hard to her,
and still she hated the One who always loved her.

Secretly she rejoiced as the child tore through,
mouth and legs open, head thrown back, spine arched.

And the One crying, there is no other God.
And the child crying, there is no other God.

III   (And the Birds Too Pecked the Flesh)

And the birds too pecked the flesh of the fruit.
And their eyes were opened. And they would not

go near the man and woman. And ants ate
the fruit. And deer. And the seeds of the fruit

passed through them and dropped a new language over
the garden. And the garden was transformed,

digested, shat out, growing again and eaten
again. The small world made greater. And the tree

died and was remade and drifted like mold
spores, like mud on the back of the dog, like dust

itself. And all life fled the man and woman.
Scurrying, disappearing into the ground, the feet

and mouths, clawing, digging, chewing—and fruit
like rotting eyes dropping from the trees.

IV   (If You Are an Angel)

If you are an angel, I am the wind.
If you are a shepherd, I am a wolf.

If you a bomb, I am the emptiness inside.
If you are a rope, I'll descend your rough

fibers, I'll climb down into my own bones
where you are afraid to enter. Though they

open the book of my body: cranium,
breasts, the catacombs of lungs, scroll of the tongue,

pearl ovaries—you cannot read it.
However much you scream, whatever fire,

I will be beyond you, and earth is
beyond you, and the first and the last,

beyond you, and beyond you, I know,
even beyond you, there is—

V   (Where We Lived Then, Circle)

Where we lived then, circle, arc of tenderness,
a place we could keep moving but never

get lost, all that time you didn't hear me,
or was it the other way around? Maybe

my sky was an eggshell, my god a great bird,
my home a nest of spit. Ending where I

began. It's just another failure, like
the spider's eggs wrapped in silk, blown into

the mud. Like obedience, its red slash
of loss. Lately, when I'm sleeping, an animal

wakes inside me, volcanic at the base
of my throat. Long-limbed, cramped by my ribs.

Deep groans, a song inside a song. Changes
are coming, my lambs, start your roaring.

VI   *(Something Long Forgotten)*

Something long forgotten comes into her.
Some days she thinks the afterbirth still drags

behind her, her breasts hard with milk. She clears
a place, setting stones for a garden. Now

all that was buried comes back. Earth bursting
with memory. And each flower pulling her face

inside its face. The legs of spring scissored
open. And the heaving. When it gets so bad

she wants to die, she tries to remember.
To get past the nostalgia for submission,

past surrender, law, altar, the rape
of the divine. Spring scissors inside her.

The marching, the soldiers, children with guns,
something long forgotten comes into her.

VII (*I Wore Night like a Glove*)

I wore night like a glove so I could be unknown
to you, held by black threads, all my light

a spitting candle, a wandering eye within.
Sometimes I catch myself waiting for

betrayal. Genetic code of blame and what
I don't have to be because I am hurt.

I think we have to do this together. Healing
into the deepest part of the wound

where bone shows through and the bleeding
can't be stopped. Past naming and the branch

of the tongue. Past the red gelatin of fear.
Let's worship just the breath that pumps us

to life and leaves us tasting death. Breathe into me
love, so I can feel you enter, feel you leave.

VIII (Look, My Side Splits with Joy)

Look, my side splits with joy as if I could draw
the rib out of myself. Some days I'm just

a gate opening and closing. Or a pond
and someone swimming to the surface. Some days

you are listening, but not always. I was
a cell and a rodent. A seahorse and a horse.

And you? We were grass and moss, wasp and
the paper house. I was grotto, painted cave,

canals salty and webbed. You were sometimes
everything. When I come through here again,

will you be waiting? A root underground, a tuber,
a stone. Even if everything is wrong,

will you know me? I've never been able
to tell anyone, really, who I am.

IX   (We Keep Trying to Pinpoint)

We keep trying to pinpoint the beginning.
Was it when someone wanted to live forever?

In the common story it starts with a bang,
one instant, one nothing, but when it un-

ravels, explodes, stone to mountain, rain to
sea, constellations of cells...garden

of space, how many flowers blink there,
how many trees carry galaxies on

their backs. Let the mind be broken, like a star
on the earth, space streaming into my mouth.

Though someone still needs comfort: yes, darling,
forever, heaven, hell, and all of that,

beyond ten thousand suns, I'll still know you,
where we began, and keep beginning.

X   (It's Just the Starting Place)

It's just the starting place, a hollow in
the grass, a place to lay myself under

the tree. I was made here, this is my home.
I tell this to the two mouths of my body

and the rivers between them. Paradise
is the body become a lens for the light

to rush through, silver flesh, phosphorus bones.
The planet turning inward to know itself.

I leave everything I have to you—dirt
and dust. Make what you can of me. I was

born here, return me to grass lullabies,
the black tea of creation. O broken-rib earth,

red orb in the tree, I touch you, my fruit,
my flesh. I eat you, my forbidden.

XI   (What If One Has to Go On)

What if one has to go on without the other?
What if paradise is the lake of loss

where each thing is baptized: the boat of the body,
clouds, rain, stones? Overhead the trees' crowns

snapping at the sky. Too late to learn to serve
the gangly plant, too late to resow ourselves.

Stupid species, your parents let things go
too far. Remember the economics of death?

I leave you my tons of waste, dear one.
My collections: knives, photos, curtains,

clocks, mirrors, my electronic name.
Endangered bees rage in the wisteria.

Loss of pollinators and their honey—
that gold soup made of sex and light.

XII   *(Paradise Came over Me Once)*

Paradise came over me once. A grove
of tall eucalyptus trees, long red leaves

we picked off the ground, animals following us.
His voice echoing among the trees, naming

everything, filling the silence with brittle
kingdoms: moon-faced owls, finches, a dead mouse,

core of an apple. He couldn't stop himself.
I mocked him: earlobe, nipple, throat. He floated

from me, brooding like the huge trees with their
gigantic solitude. I turned away.

For a long time we had been enough: what I'd
later name happiness. Sweet kernel within

my despair. Don't ask why. Think of your own hunger,
how it gets worse no matter what you feed it.

XIII   *(If You Breathe in the Long Sentence)*

If you breathe in the long sentence of the wind,
it will run down along your spine, your ancient

cliff, layered, eon on eon: orange,
ochre, white: sand, crystal: into the body's

rockface. Compressed ladder of the past you can't
get down, your mind laboring to bore through bone

but stuck hovering above where there's always
an odor of veiled knowledge and confusion.

Weren't you back there once? Didn't you taste it?
Clamp it, long ago, between your legs? Now this

whirlpool of debris and amnesia. Creatures of
the second day gone, and the third. When asked you say:

I don't know, as if to open a well inside,
a place the lost world could rise into, and fill.

XIV   (Still, the Red Rag of Desire)

Still, the red rag of desire, even after
so many years, fending off the lords of

shut-up and kneel down. Black cat of more.
Legs have their own destination,

entanglements. And I can finally say,
I'm tired, why not? of fertility. Flesh

basket, wineskin, sponge, milk spout, swollen anchor.
Too water-soaked, lust-soaked. Birthing always

even when nothing is there, nothing
but squat and spirit, how all the answers

come like that, through a woodland womb, dense, wet
with the wind's slippery body.

Time to birth what isn't there, time to cry out,
rip open, bloody with the unknown.

XV   (The Cord Between Us)

The cord between us no one else could see.
Days only this, mother and child. Small halo

of loss and exhausted love around us.
We grew from each other, then grew apart.

Child, we cannot remake the world. This grief
will always be with us, your eyes will hurt.

You'll be taken from yourself, rushed from
your root, we'll depart unmoored. Expect

uniforms, murder. Whoever, like Abraham,
rubs your neck and leads you to the altar,

whoever asks you to choose and bow down,
will be against you. Loyalty to what?

Before this world went wrong, we were worshipped.
And the cracked egg of earth. Remember? Worshipped.

XVI   (Of All the Species)

Of all the species, this primate broke through.
Exalted itself, worshipped, knew less, knew more.

One word came forth. A machete, axe, bronze
spear shot out such news as rose us up,

as hurtled us forward, wherever our feet
could take us. Glean the berries, skin hides, pretend

to be a fox or bear, or long sleek snake.
The great voice says, You. The towers say, You.

Trains rush from the mouth: You, You. Ships of You.
Where's Eden? A place we must not enter.

Shroud of forest cover, mist, no cameras.
If we wander in by mistake they have

no fear of us and approach us. Dominion
was not the first dream; it is not the last.

XVII   *(In the Dream, My Son)*

In the dream, my son, drowning, and I lift
him out of the water, my arms around

his chest squeezing him so his lungs will open.
And dragging him toward the others, screaming

bring him back, bring him back, the musculature
of fear a vise around me and me around

my son. No one hears, though I scream on,
a useless tongue, screaming on—

I wake up. Stunned and beating. He's away,
his bed empty, a hole in the house,

too many terrors meeting here. My feet
still in the lake of the dream. Then

prayer or anything that might shake the stain
from me, *leave us alone*, I weep, or, *drown me.*

XVIII   *(Mid-summer, Anything Can Be Bruised)*

Mid-summer, anything can be bruised if you
touch it wrong. Purple figs. Tomato plant

fallen over; when I try to lift it
I break the branch. Near me the hummingbird's

motor. Sunflowers' golden hands, palms up.
At Jane's I walk past a grove of orange trees.

Walk through tall grass and around the stone wall
to pick one. Gouge thin skin with my thumbnail,

peel the orange, dripping, eat it standing
next to the tree. A short tree so I bend

toward it. The first one makes me ravenous.
Juice all over. I have never done this before.

Drenching myself with my hunger, eating
more oranges, in love with my hunger.

XIX   (Now That You Are Dead)

Now that you are dead and I slowly unfold
my package of fear, I hardly tell anyone

or myself, about being owned. Girl on the wheel
and you throwing your knives, just missing me.

Such wounds in the air. What's mercy? Me leaving?
Your footsteps in the garden, a vigilante

recording my phone calls? Mercy—a blank
firmament that has no finish line,

that doesn't lay claim with its hammer
and nails? Some days now I'm unafraid,

as if nothing could touch me, or what touched me
was nothing. Forgiveness is another country.

The black eye of a bird, or its small feet. Another
country. Far off. Continent. Cloud.

XX   (The Words Were Ambrosia)

The words were ambrosia, a bowl of wild
strawberries. You said you knew where some grew

and had picked them right in New York City.
The size of red tears. Vowels of paradise

here in a bowl on the balcony. You said
you knew where some grew and they were hidden

and wild at the same time in the city.
Said you couldn't describe the taste, more like

fragrance melting on the tongue, filling
your head. You knew where they still grew, hidden,

though we had a bowl of them then and there
on a balcony, overlooking the garden.

Wild strawberries, small pearls of forgetfulness,
in another country, above a garden.

XXI   *(A Scratchy Radio Voice Whispers)*

A scratchy radio voice whispers *the waters*
are coming. Noah hears it and gathers

his own, says, *Don't think about them drowning*
in the deluge, we did what we could.

See Noah wave from his plane, smiling like
God's own secret above the broken levees,

below him the whole world a sick brown sea,
survivors begging from roofs, bodies

floating, cars in the trees. Days of pleading
of please God, days of the discarded,

the great eyes and ears shut. Meanwhile
Father Noah talks rapture and big bucks—

says he's connected to the higher-ups,
he has Dominion, a Plan, a wind-up dove.

XXII   (Gold Littering Sidewalks)

Gold littering sidewalks, fire falling
from branches. Autumn's last rush when I

feel stripped, undone as a tree heading
toward its long sleep, unable to escape.

When the trees shake and burn to their essence
grief comes on me sudden and deep. Don't tell me

to rise above it. Don't say the body's
a ladder, start climbing. I'm rubbing myself

in ash; I'm down to gristle and ember.
I don't think I can go any farther.

Grasses afire, crackling in the wind.
Leaves raining from volcanic trees, it's the day

before the last day, before the last day.
I'm burning my stem, my shell, my seed.

XXIII   (Now, Believing Only in What No One)

Now, believing only in what no one
has told me, I climb to the room where Clare

died, unable to explain why I kneel
for the dead saint on the cold stone floor,

or why I pray—and to whom and for what?
My right eye weeping, my left looking out

at the cloak of blue sky. Her last words on the wall:
the one who created me has ever

cared for me, as a mother her
tiny baby. Then rowing across her

milk lake, on a boat made of flesh. Rowing
out of exile toward another country.

Tender froth. All that was forgotten
coming back, written in milk ink, blood ink.

XXIV   (Who Comes to Me?)

Who comes to me? Who enters the room where
I have been praying, longing for a visitor?

Holy virus, holy host. Through air, touch
of the hand, a sip for the driest lips—

who comes? Thou who so loved the world, thou gave
thrashing, delirium, gave fever in

the hearth, gave bloody. Holy is the virus
and holy its host. Fathers, mothers,

holy ghost. Holy is the virus laying
low the host. Sons, daughters, holy ghost.

Who comes to me? Lover, friend....
Who enters the cell where I have been praying,

longing for a visitor? Who comes to me
through air, touch, a sip for the driest lips—

XXV   (Empty It, All of It)

Empty it, all of it, that's the only way.
Too many words. Now I hear all music

exiting earth, lifting off—the buses
below, lifting—traffic, lifting. I came

for this, to raise up the rock of sound
and find what's underneath. What lives there in

the dirt, without light. I came here for no one.
White towels folded on the tub, books and shoes

scattered. It's good to be unknown, a stranger,
good to know nothing and no one and say *now, now*,

and sleep and walk, and sleep and open all
the drawers and swing wide the oversized door

stepping inside. Dear No One, in the closet
of emptiness, all the clothes are yours.

XXVI   (In the Beginning Was the Animal)

In the beginning was the animal
of space licking earth to life, the night sky

lit with great herds of stars, and the paths of planets
growing radiant rubbing each other.

Heaven's thrust and caress upon us,
green and fertile in the cracks, poultice of dust,

spore, pollen and ash. Creation's luminous
mouth. In the beginning all that was made

was good because it was made, and what was
made and not-made knew each other, and it

was good. The stars in unending intercourse.
Heaven an amnio sac, the slopping

salty center, from there all the swimmers
breaststroking, diving, all night long, toward earth.

XXVII   (Such Was Our Luck)

Such was our luck in the teeming world, all things
coupling, all the soft membranes, thinning,

food for the underlife back when dominion
was just a dream, a word. Said casually

at first. Simple bubble. Simple speck of
a brain. Is there afterlife for the extinct?

Or is it that nothing lasts but tries on
the endless forms. The madmen line up for

horseshoes, ringers, and call for time's end.
Stupid species. Severing the planet's cord.

Umbilical space sings us its eerie songs.
Go, make weapons while you dream about heaven.

Bomb anything that moves; that's what you love
isn't it? Torture? Screams? Someone begging to die?

XXVIII   *(What I Wake To)*

What I wake to in the layered winter bed,
and fall back into in the sling of sleep,

and walk around all day, in and out of.
Beneath the papery skin around my eyes

another life. Snow, gray and brittle, the sky
sagging so low it might be a rag around

my head. Thoughts—cold, sharp—dirty ice crackling
at the edge of the walk. Unrest inside,

the unseen trying to stir the frozen
underworld. I don't say it. The white roots

inside me, winter-glazed. I don't say it.
And even when everything is at risk,

sore with longing, I don't say it, and soon
it carves a space inside me with its absence.

XXIX (We Traveled as Seeds and Dust Travel)

We traveled as seeds and dust travel, by wind
or bird, spread to all corners, we were desire

exhausting itself, a membrane shuddering.
Was it accident brought us together?

I remember you as I first saw you, bent over,
studying something, just your back and the top

of your head. I still see your shoulders' hunch
and hunger. Your body like some great

plant struggling from earth. And how to speak—
wasn't there a strange language, something deep

from the dirt of our throats? Each day we try to wake up,
but it's late now in the common story.

We come from pollen tongue, spider weed,
from the blue rib of sea, dropped here, dreaming.

XXX   *(Octave to Octave She Passes)*

Octave to octave she passes through the hole
in the world, gathering our weeping into

her voice, as if the cantata were cancer
made song, the beauty of loss swarming us.

On stage in hospital gown and socks, IV
hanging from her arm, she is what she'll become,

a woman not wanting to die, and all
that applause, audience crying—stay with us,

don't leave—flowers flung at her. I think her death
unreal, unable to believe in the voice

without the mouth as it comes through my headphones
burning a trail inside me. Time to let go,

time to get ready in all the salt pockets
of grief, singing, stay with me, don't leave.

for Lorraine Hunt Lieberson
1954-2006

XXXI   (No, Earth Is an Eye Unhitched)

No, earth is an eye unhitched, spinning from
a fine bright tail, a blue and white swirled gaze.

Or down here earth is ochre, the late blinding
sun staring her down as she crosses the old bridge,

the city doubled in the river. She limps
through Florence as some pilgrims limp, thrown by

the slant of light but still searching. All day
saints splayed on walls, their painted mouths open

like spouts, till she's seen, and not seen, enough,
and pilgrimed enough across the bone ridge

asking for a sign. And earth, unhitched, spinning,
is an eye out of its socket. Driven mad.

Clothes soaked with the heat. Burning river
and faces, burning light, all things shining.

XXXII (And as to the Planet, Also to Her)

And as to the planet, also to her—
from the rutted, coiled, earth-body, through the road

where they passed at will, a radio blasting
its backwards prayer. Also visions, fragments—

clavicles, arms, burnt tires, a yellowed
torn dress. Her legs spread. Here is where

they entered, where they left. Birth blood gathering
at the roadside, reports stacked on the desk. Then what.

Ropes, pulleys, wires. She feels herself a stone
someone picked up and thought to throw, but held tight

instead. And the stone is not the center. Nor fist,
nor womb, nor she, the center. Sucked into

the dark hive of matter. Weary past where
the body ever was, sucked down, mother, down.

XXXIII   *(If You Believe in Ice and Thaw)*

If you believe in ice and thaw, in fields,
woodlands, in leaves falling where they were always

meant to fall, like hands clasped around trunks
and along gullies, the road swerving toward

nowhere. If you believe in a secret north
luring these thousands of Snow Geese, their

blue and white underwings above our heads.
If you believe you'll be called again to

the carnal belly, that you'll answer the failing
light with your reed mouth, crying like the geese,

feathers growing stiff on your throat, a flight
into grit and dirt, home of silt, water,

abandoned oval shells—I'll be
with you—with you unto the last shelter.

XXXIV   (Darwin Came Seasick into Paradise)

Darwin came seasick into paradise.
Packing the ship with crates of fossils, plants,

dead birds, anything he could kill or dig up.
Five years collecting, ten to sift through it all.

And in the brain's bright cell a viscous
humming, the terrible doubts. Later, when

the favored child died, when she moved through
the first wilderness without him, Annie

decomposing into chalky layers—
no comfort. Just hymns of transmutation,

songs of barnacles, earthworms, finches, and
the lonely tortoise. We are parasites

inside parasites, and some have wings. Annie
on shore, as he lurched seasick into paradise.

XXXV   (After Ages of Watching Over)

After ages of watching over, of shearing
and slaughter, we lay down in the field to the echoes

and tremors of sheep yanking the rough grass.
Soon, we dreamed we'd become the grass that the sheep

gripped with their small teeth, slowly chewing us
from the hairs of our legs to the flesh of our bellies,

picking at our ribs, warm breath grazing
our hearts. The sheep ate the delicacy

of eyes and cheeks. And when our skulls' seams
cracked open, flying things descended

on our remains. Too late to wake up.
Easy to let go. Torn to bits with no

tongues left to thank them. Given at last
to the happiness, that we had long forgotten.

XXXVI   (She Heads into the Wilderness)

She heads into the wilderness, weeping
and stunned by shame, her eyes open. Into

another country, bent and becoming,
fibrous and heavy in her body, feeling

that she is the tree, or that she is the fruit
that ripens and falls, that falls and will keep

falling her whole life. As if all that mattered
was plummeting to earth and splitting open.

And who hasn't stumbled out of herself
into the body of suffering? Into

bare flesh, stooped shoulders, and the dark hole
of the mouth. Threats still ringing, and that taste

she never forgot, taste with no end, world with
no end. Gates fading, the wind shushing her on.

_____ **THREE**

Epilogue

_____ The Long Drive

Through the prism and sap
of scruff pine, its thick
tongue, its sawtooth, and
the woods layered with stripes,

I've seen the small patch
of nowhere, its low brush and
sandy bottom, overhead
all the wings circling. I drive

past and catch sight—
a hollow of light running down
the trees toward a woman,
myself, standing alone.

Each time I glance, each new
mile, I'm out there between
tree trunks, watching
myself drive by.

_____ The Painted Quilt

What does it mean, decorative?
The way cells cluster? Minerals crystallize?

And the painted quilt? Red pattern where

the fireplace should be, tiles with
iotas of difference, shapes poised against

each other—the way of geometry.

I count myself as plane and volume,
as part of the shapes pinwheeling

toward me—sequences, codes, rows

of triangles, unhinged stars teetering
on their points. I study the painted quilt,

its colors of iron and gold, its shapes

evolved to pattern, to see how we are made
in the image of octagon, spiral,

the shapes in my face or yours.

When I die, let the painted quilt with
its arrowheads, its starry hub, rest

above me. First beauty of things. How

the patterns flashed before us but we forgot
how to see them. Tonight, I count

the strange message of July's cobalt sky,

count as if backwards to before my birth,
backward before Euclid, before grass, slate,

before shape, line, toward light, backward,
forward, counting toward

the unknown numbers that made us.

Torso

And the silver torso, where
the ghost lives. And the torso
of gold and mud. Whatever else,
all her days missing, all
her work gone, the torso
and her upturned collar,
a span, a bridge, twisted—

and the grass around it,
and the torso, standing.

What makes the spirits come
to live here, after all we've
done to them? What makes
the grass and brush try to tangle
itself in knots and the half-body
to rise up, to turn toward us
as we come into the field?

_____ The Changing Coat

When I wake up, heart
up my throat, a fear taste—
getting ready for
the changing skin.

Your hat on the knob
of the banister, tilted.
You ask, _why are you
holding up your head_

with your hand? I'm tired,
stripped down, maybe
I passed one of my deaths
getting ready for

the changing skin.
Sometimes, love, I can be
your sister, dead,
come to you in her

changing skin—tortoise
shell eyes, through gravel
and moss. And you can be
my brother, dead, saying:

I never meant to hurt anyone.
We are looking across
the table. It's a field,
long, spread out, pale,

the ground's icy. We're wearing
our new coats and we've passed
one or more of our deaths
along the way. There's no

afterlife, it's the same, the
same life, and when
we remember that we pull
close our changing coats,

we tilt toward each other,
the ground is softer
than I thought,
our foreheads touch.

_____ The Bee's Coat

Wax and spit and hair.

Pollen to glow.

Make me something to wear

with room for wings.

I want the splendor coat—

wax, spit, and hair.

Gold dust. It's not too late

to burrow in the cup,

to chew and spin. A simple coat,

pollen-matted, trailing light.

I want to shine in this world.

——— My Lost Needle

Never had I desire to mend
        hems or dangling buttons,

but tonight, though I can no longer
        easy aim the frayed end

into the eye, though we squint,
        needle and I, at each other,

and my hand trembles, yet feels true
        the needle between my fingers,

the tether of thread as I pull it
        through red linen, just the right

turn in my wrist, not too fast, thread
        rubbing the blouse, repeating

mend, mend, my dearest, hold fast, let me
        patch you, no one will know,

you limp in my hand, draped on my lap,
        my other body. I with

my warm, fine instrument, you undone,
        never whole without me.

I would sew till the world around wore
        patches bright and uneven,

sew my childhood back into my bones,
        I would bind, I would bind

what falls apart. My hand is happy—
        piercing, rising, circling back—

taking me thou needle, thou red thread,
        stitch to stitch, my way back,

taking there, and I go, what more
        wanting, what more?

Notes

From: "Their Eyes Were Opened"

IX "The common story" is from Sallie McFague's *The Body of God.* "The common creation story...is the story of everything that is, of how the universe began fifteen billion years ago and how it evolved into some hundred billion galaxies of which our Milky Way is one." (27)

XVI *(Of All the Species)* The first line comes out of E. O. Wilson's essay, "Is Humanity Suicidal?" "Darwin's dice have rolled badly for Earth. It was a misfortune for the living world in particular...that a carnivorous primate and not some more benign form of animal made the breakthrough." *In Search of Nature* (184)

"Dominion" from Genesis 2:26: "And God said, Let us make man in our image, after our likeness: and let them have dominion over the fish of the sea, and over the fowl of the air, and over the cattle, and over all the earth, and over every creeping thing that creepeth upon the earth." *King James Bible*

XXI *(A Scratchy Radio Voice Whispered)* is for the victims of Hurricane Katrina.

XXIII "Clare" is Clare of Assisi at San Damiano, the convent where she lived and died.

"The Painted Quilt" is inspired by and dedicated to the artist Erica Haba.

"The Bee's Coat" is for my brother, Joseph Macari.

"Torso" and "The Changing Coat" are inspired by and dedicated to the artist Martha Posner.

I wish to thank Joan Larkin and Jean Valentine, without whom I can't imagine having written this book. Also, Jan Heller Levi and Alicia Ostriker for reading these poems so closely and for their excellent advice. Gerald Stern for unflagging belief and for being my first and last reader. My sons, Noah, Lukas, and Jeremy Musher for true support and encouragement. Lukas also for his love and deep knowledge of birds and the natural world, which has inspired and informed me in these poems.

I also am grateful to Michael Simms and Autumn House Press for their kindness and support of this book.

——— The Autumn House Poetry Series

Michael Simms, Executive Editor

Snow White Horses, Selected Poems 1973–88 by Ed Ochester

The Leaving, New and Selected Poems by Sue Ellen Thompson

Dirt by Jo McDougall

Fire in the Orchard by Gary Margolis

Just Once, New and Previous Poems by Samuel Hazo

The White Calf Kicks by Deborah Slicer ● 2003, selected by
    Naomi Shihab Nye

The Divine Salt by Peter Blair

The Dark Takes Aim by Julie Suk

Satisfied with Havoc by Jo McDougall

Half Lives by Richard Jackson

Not God After All by Gerald Stern (with drawings by Sheba Sharrow)

Dear Good Naked Morning by Ruth L. Schwartz ● 2004,
    selected by Alicia Ostriker

A Flight to Elsewhere by Samuel Hazo

Collected Poems by Patricia Dobler

The Autumn House Anthology of Contemporary American Poetry,
    edited by Sue Ellen Thompson

Déjà Vu Diner by Leonard Gontarek

Lucky Wreck by Ada Limon ● 2005, selected by Jean Valentine

The Golden Hour by Sue Ellen Thompson

Woman in the Painting by Andrea Hollander Budy

Joyful Noise: An Anthology of American Spiritual Poetry,
    edited by Robert Strong

No Sweeter Fat by Nancy Pagh ● 2006, selected by Tim Seibles

Unreconstructed: Poems Selected and New by Ed Ochester

Rabbis of the Air by Philip Terman

Let It Be a Dark Roux: New and Selected Poems by Sheryl St. Germain

Dixmont by Rick Campbell

The River Is Rising by Patricia Jabbeh Wesley

The Dark Opens by Miriam Levine ● 2007, selected by Mark Doty

The Song of the Horse by Samuel Hazo

My Life as a Doll by Elizabeth Kirschner

She Heads into the Wilderness by Anne Marie Macari

● winner of the annual Autumn House Press Poetry Prize

——— Design and Production

Cover and text design by Kathy Boykowycz
Cover art: detail of ancient Egyptian wall painting

Text set in ITC Officina Sans, designed by Erik Spiekermann in 1990
Section titles set in Skia, designed by Matthew Carter

Printed by Thomson-Shore of Dexter, Michigan,
on Nature's Natural, a 50% recycled paper